BASIC BIBLE PRIMER

I learn to read

about Jesus

by Leilah E. Runyon

Illustrated by

June Kallmeyer Deist

STANDARD PUBLISHING
CINCINNATI, OHIO

FOLLOWING A TRADITION

The new Basic Bible Readers are a beautiful, up-to-date edition of the famous Standard Bible Story Readers, by Lillie A. Faris, that were first printed in 1925. More than a million copies have been added to the libraries of homes, schools, and churches in the past four decades.

The best of the former readers has been retained in this new series, including the favorite Bible stories that forever appeal to our children. However, all of the illustrations are completely new—drawn by noted children's artists of today. A primer for the beginning reader has been added to the series.

Introduction

I Learn to Read About Jesus is a Bible primer for the beginning reader who is in the first grade. In public school the child is having the happy experience of reading for himself. Parents and Bible-school teachers may add to this pleasure and take advantage of the child's eagerness to read by providing him with Bible story books that he can read for himself. This Basic Bible Primer is such a book. Although not all children learn at the same rate, an average reader will know all except the new Bible words by the end of the first semester in first grade. The number of Bible words already learned will be determined by the child's religious background.

The picture on each page was carefully planned to introduce visually the new Bible words. The relation of pictures to words is re-emphasized by the illustrated word list on pages 58 and 59. Even before the child begins to read the stories, he may learn the unfamiliar Bible words by reading the illustrated word list with the help of an adult.

After the child has read the stories, he may review the new words by using the word list on page 61. The list on pages 62 and 63 includes all of the words in this book. It is provided to give the beginning reader additional help with even the basic secular words. The child may review the pronunciation of these words by reading them in this list, then review their meanings by reading them again in their context.

While this primer will probably be most used in the home, it is valuable for the Bible school too. Copies should be in the church library so that teachers and parents may borrow them for reference or for inspection in deciding what to buy. The teacher may place the book on the reading table for use before class or in free Bible activity time. If several copies are available, the teacher may like to have the class read together some of the stories. Or sections may be copied on a reading chart or chalkboard for the class to read together.

—*the Editor.*

I Learn To Read About Jesus

STORIES

The Baby Jesus

Look, look!
Look and see.
See the baby.
See baby Jesus.

Look and see.
See the mother.
Mary is the mother.

Look, look!
See baby Jesus.
See the mother.
See baby Jesus and Mary.

Look, look!
See the manger.
The baby is in the manger.
See the baby and the manger.

Look and see.
See Bethlehem.
The manger is in Bethlehem.
Baby Jesus is in Bethlehem.
Mary is in Bethlehem.

Look, look!
Sheep, sheep.
See the sheep.
See the white sheep on the hill.

Shepherds, shepherds.
Look and see.
See the shepherds.
See the shepherds on the hill.

Look, look.
Look and see.
See the shepherds and the
white sheep on the hill.

Look, look.
Look and see.
See the angel.
See the shepherds.

The angel said,
"Go, go. Go and see.
See the baby.
See the King.
Baby Jesus is the King."

The angel said,
"Baby Jesus is in Bethlehem.
Baby Jesus is in the manger.
Go and see."

The shepherds go
to see the baby,
to see the baby Jesus.
Baby Jesus is the King.

The shepherds go
to see the King,
to see the baby Jesus.
Jesus is in Bethlehem.
The shepherds go to Bethlehem.

See baby Jesus in the manger.
See Mary.
See the shepherds.
The shepherds see baby Jesus.

Jesus is the King.

Jesus is God's little boy.

The shepherds see Jesus.

The shepherds see the King.

The shepherds see God's little boy.

The shepherds said,
"We saw angels.
The angels said,
'Go to Bethlehem.
Go and see the baby Jesus.
Go and see the King.'"

The shepherds said,
"We saw the King.
We saw God's little boy.
We saw baby Jesus
in the manger."

The Wise-men

Look, look!
See the star.
Look and see the star.
See the star go.

The Wise-men look.
The Wise-men see the star.

Go, Wise-men, go.
Go to see baby Jesus.
Baby Jesus is the King.

The Wise-men see the star.
The Wise-men go to Jerusalem
to see the baby King.

Baby Jesus is the King.
Baby Jesus is God's little boy.

The Wise-men said,
"Where is the baby King?
We saw the star.
Where is the baby King?"

King Herod is in Jerusalem.

The Wise-men said to King Herod,
"Where? Where?
Where is the baby King?"

King Herod said,
"Go, Wise-men, go.
Go to Bethlehem.
The baby King is in Bethlehem.
Go and see the baby King,
Then come and tell me."

The Wise-men go.
The Wise-men go to Bethlehem.
The Wise-men see the star.

See the star go.

"Go, star, go.
Take us to Bethlehem.
Help us find baby Jesus.
Find the baby King."

Go, Wise-men, go.
Go to Bethlehem.
Find baby Jesus.
Find the baby King.
Find God's little boy.

Here is Bethlehem.
Here is the star.
Here is the house.
Let us see.

Look, Wise-men, look!
Here is the mother, Mary.
Here is the baby Jesus.
He is the King.

"This is something for the baby."

"This is something for baby Jesus."

"This is something for God's little boy—something for the King."

Jesus is the King!
The Wise-men saw the baby King.
The Wise-men are happy.
Now the Wise-men can go home.

The Boy Jesus

Now Jesus is a big boy.
Jesus is 12 years old.
1, 2, 3, 4, 5, 6, 7, 8,
9, 10, 11, 12.
Jesus is 12 years old.

To Jerusalem
Jesus is going.
Joseph is going.
Mary is going.
All three are going to Jerusalem.

Fathers are going.
Mothers are going.
Big boys are going.
They all are going to Jerusalem.

This is the temple.
The temple is God's house.
The temple is in Jerusalem.

Fathers go to the temple.
Mothers go to the temple.
Big boys go to the temple.
Jesus is a big boy.
Jesus is going to the temple.

Jesus is God's boy.
Jesus comes to the temple.
Jesus comes to God's house.
God's house is the temple.

Here is the Bible.
The Bible is God's book.
God's book is in God's house.
God's book is in the temple.

Jesus sees the teachers.
The teachers are in God's house.

The teachers read God's book.
God's book is the Bible.

Jesus loves God's book.
Jesus loves God's house.
Jesus talks with the teachers.
They read God's book.

1, 2, 3, 4, 5, 6, 7—seven days.
The fathers are in Jerusalem.
The mothers are in Jerusalem.
The big boys are in Jerusalem.
All are in Jerusalem seven days.

Now they go home.
The fathers go home.
The mothers go home.
The big boys go home.

Mary said, "Where is Jesus?
Jesus is not here."

Joseph said, "Where is Jesus?
Jesus is not here.
We must find Jesus."

Mary said to the mothers,
"Is Jesus here?"

Joseph said to the fathers,
"Is Jesus here?"

They said to the big boys,
"Is Jesus here?"

They all said,
"No. Jesus is not here."

Where is Jesus?

1, 2, 3—three days
Joseph looks for Jesus.
Mary looks for Jesus.
They look three days.

They look and look.
Then they go to the temple.
They go to the teachers.

Here is Jesus.
Here is God's book.
Here are the teachers.
They are in God's house.

Mary said, "Jesus, we
have looked for you.
Come with us now.
Come home with us."

Jesus said,
"God is my Father.
I must do what
He tells me to do."

Jesus is going with Mary and Joseph.

Jesus is a good boy.

Jesus is God's boy.

He will do what God tells Him to do.

Jesus

Mary

Bethlehem

manger

sheep

shepherds

angel

God's boy

star

Wise-men

King Herod

Jerusalem

Joseph

temple

Bible

teachers

For Mother and Father

After your child has read the stories in this book, by all means read them to him directly from the Bible The references are given below.

Reading these stories to the child from the Bible will help to impress him with the fact that they are true stories, because they are in God's Book. And, as you read the Bible, sometimes even letting the child read with you the words he knows, your child will develop a love for God's Word and an eagerness to hear more Bible stories. Your attitude will influence your child's attitude toward the Bible, both now and in the years to come.

THE BABY JESUS
Luke 2:1-20

THE WISE-MEN
Matthew 2:1-12

THE BOY JESUS
Luke 2:41-52

New Basic Bible Vocabulary

The Basic Bible Primer: *I Learn to Read About Jesus* is the first in the series of five Basic Bible Readers.

This book contains a total of 85 different words. Of these, 68 words are repeated from public school pre-primers and primers; 17 new words are introduced and are listed below.

Page

Page

6. Jesus

7. Mary

8. . . .

9. manger

10. Bethlehem

11. sheep

12. shepherds

13. . . .

14. angel

15. King

16. . . .

17. . . .

18. . . .

19. . . .

20. God's

21. . . .

22. . . .

23. . . .

24. star

25. Wise-men

26. Jerusalem

27. . . .

28. Herod

29. . . .

30. . . .

31. . . .

32. . . .

33. . . .

34. . . .

35. . . .

36. . . .

37. . . .

38. . . .

39. Joseph

40. . . .

41. temple

42. . . .

43. . . .

44. Bible

45. teachers

Complete Primer Word List

The following list includes every word used in the Basic Bible Primer: *I Learn to Read About Jesus.*

Page

6. look
   and
   see
   the
   baby
   Jesus
7. mother
   Mary
   is
8. . . .
9. manger
   in
10. Bethlehem
11. sheep
   white
   on
   hill
12. shepherds
13. . . .
14. angel
15. said
   go
   King
16. . . .

Page

17. to
18. . . .
19. . . .
20. God's
   little
   boy
21. we
   saw
22. . . .
23. . . .
24. star
25. Wise-men
26. Jerusalem
27. where
28. Herod
29. then
   come
   tell
   me
30. . . .
31. take
   us
   help
   find